This Book Belongs to

_____

MY HORSE WITH A PINK BOW

Copyright © 2022 by Barbara Burgess

ISBN 13: 978-1-7368216-4-0
Library of Congress PCN: 2002906266

All Rights Reserved. No parts of this book may be reproduced or utilized in any form or by any means, electronic or mechanical, including photocopying, scanning, recording, or by any information storage and retrieval system now known or hereafter invented, without permission, in writing from the publisher.

To order a copy of this book,
please visit www.amitypublications.com

Design and Layout by
AMITY Publications

Printed in the United States of America

MY HORSE WITH A PINK BOW

Written by Barbara Burgess
Illustrated by Joel Burgess

DEDICATION

To my husband Ken Burgess
who died before his grandchildren were born.
He would have been one of their favorite
horses to ride, too!

To my family, friends and all the staff
at Seacoast Cancer Center, Dover, New Hampshire,
who provided excellent personal medical care and support
through my breast cancer ordeal.

SPECIAL THANK YOU

To my son, Joel Burgess,
who lived this experience and illustrated
the interpretation of my story as written.

To my grandchildren
who helped to motivate me during this journey
and whose questions inspired me to write this story.

To my publisher, Layne Case
who encouraged me to share my story with others
as a means of education, support, and hope.

My favorite horse is my Nana B.

Such fun we have when she visits me!

She's strong and fast as she gallops around

With me on her back, "Neigh" is her sound.

That's the signal...then off we go

Round the stable yard 'til I call "whoa!"

We stop for water and I feed her a cracker,

Then, "Giddy-up" again. She's no slacker!

Soon we stop to let my sister ride.

But before she gets on, she holds with pride

A big pink bow placed in Nana's hair.

She says, "I want to ride a pretty mare!"

Off they go again to faraway places.

Round and round and round she paces.

Sister grabs her mane, so silky and long,

But then one day, it was totally GONE!

"Where's all your hair? Where did it go?

And how can you wear Sister's pretty pink bow?"

We noticed she'd also slowed down quite a bit.

She would not eat; then she just QUIT!

She used to laugh and smile a lot.

So much fun when we would trot.

But then her smiles...they went away.

Even she was worried, I would say.

She said she was sick now, and needed to rest.

She went to the doctor who did lots of tests.

It made us sad to see her this way,

"When can we ride again, Nana?" we'd say.

She was poked and prodded but the nurses were nice.

They said she'd get well, and they gave her advice.

The medicine they gave her should help a lot,

But it might be awhile before she could trot.

A whole year passed by the time she got well

Before we could ride again, near as I could tell.

She ate more carrots and crackers too,

And drank lots of water as horses do.

Her hair had grown back; it was short and stumpy,

But she smiled more now and wasn't as grumpy.

Gradually her hair grew curly and long.

Over time, her legs also got strong.

Finally the day arrived, not soon enough.

We were SO excited when she visited us!

Sister could again place the pink bow in her hair.

"She's back, we can ride again!" Our Nana B mare!

October 2019

February 2020

June 2020

June 2021

April 2022

Grayson, Nana B. and Avery

For information about the BWEL Breast Cancer Study,

Visit

https://BWEL study.org

Made in the USA
Middletown, DE
12 July 2022